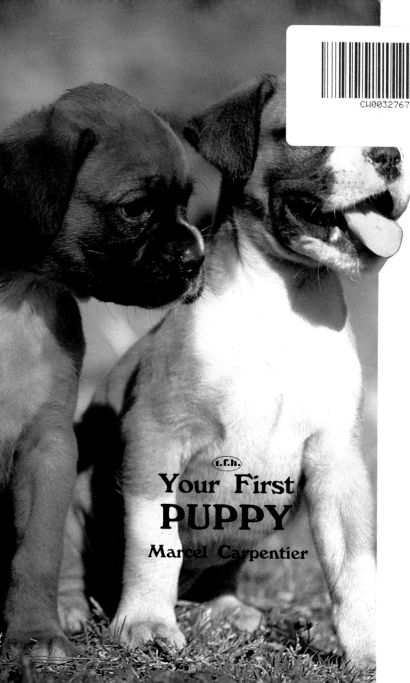

CW00327676

Bibliography

Pages 2 and 3:
Photos of boxer
puppies owned by
Richard Tomita;
photo by Isabelle
Francais.

Pages 34 and 35:
Photos of Rottweiler
puppies owned by
Deborah Gilman;
photo by Isabelle
Francais.

© 1991
By T.F.H.
Publications,
Inc., Neptune,
N.J. 07753 USA
•
T.F.H.
Publications,
The Spinney,
Parklands,
Denmead,
Portsmouth
PO7 6AR
England

Your First PUPPY

t.f.h.

Marcel Carpentier

Introduction

The subject of puppies is as big as a pup is small. Despite the dozens of breeds and countless types of mongrels, curb-setters, and mutts, all puppies share some common traits. They're lovable. They're cute. They're excusably mischievous. They're fun. They're a little child's best friend and a source of merriment and mirth for grown-ups. What better spirit-lifter-upper than a pup?

THE MANY DOGS

Although one Latin name (*Canis familiaris*) covers all domestic dogs for the purposes of zoology, there are so many varieties with so many different histories and backgrounds that it seems almost impossible to believe that they are all related. Look at a Chihuahua and then at a Great Dane. Some difference! Why? Because, in many cases, man bred them into these strange and wondrous shapes intentionally. He wanted to create dogs suitable for the various purposes for which he required them, e.g., hunting, guarding, herding, retrieving, showing, or just as friends and companions.

PICKING THE RIGHT PUPPY

How can you possibly pick one puppy from a litter of playful, tail-wagging little fellows? Take your time. Shop around. A well-kept pet shop or kennel carrying a large variety of dogs will give you an opportunity to make a good selection. Price will enter into it, of course. Pedigreed dogs cost much more than mongrels, and typically the longer their pedigree the higher their price. Many people prefer the pedigreed pup because they know what he will look like when he grows up.

Mongrels may resemble neither of their parents—but so what? They are just as faithful and loyal, even if they do make it hard to guess how big they'll grow or what they'll look like.

Unless you intentionally plan to breed or show dogs, forget about which sex is better. People who own males insist that their dogs make the better pets; people who own females are equally certain about theirs. There are too many differences in the personalities of the individual dogs to be able to generalize. Look for an active puppy, one who rolls and romps over his brothers and sisters. This is not a hard-bound rule, however. A sad-eyed shy pup, once he's out of his litter and getting your undivided attention, may blossom beautifully.

PUREBRED DOGS

Admittedly, a mongrel or mixed-breed dog can be a wonderful companion for any owner who is willing to provide the right kind of home; however, purebred dogs have strong followings and there are many, many reasons for wanting a purebred dog as a companion. By purebred we mean a dog whose sire and dam (father and mother) belong to the same breed of dog and both possess known parentages. Purebred dogs produce dogs that look similar to themselves while mutts do not pass on their physical attributes to their progeny with any reliability.

The advantages of purebred dogs go beyond the possibility of showing the dog in exhibition or showing off the dog to your friends—though both of these are possible, of course. More often than not, purebred dogs have been developed by man for specific purposes, and owners today can still rely on these dogs to perform specialized functions. Therefore, if you want a hunting companion, any member of the sporting dog or hound group will perform more successfully than a mixed-breed dog, though some mutts are great at hunting nevertheless. Or, if you want a dog to work on the farm or ranch, a purebred herding dog makes the best choice. The appearance as well as the temperament of these animals is ensured by their pedigree—theoretically. The patience and even-temperedness of the gun dogs and the large flock guardians, for instance, can be matched against any dog; while the scrappiness and outgoingness of the terriers and herding dogs, in general, outmatch even the most wiley of mongrels.

Let us briefly consider the different groups of purebred dogs; these groups are established by the dog-registering organizations for the purposes of exhibition. Thus, the hound dogs compete against the hound dogs in the show ring. For the most part, members of each group have similar characteristics and abilities.

Sporting Dogs: The sporting dogs are essentially those dogs which work from the hunter's gun. They are spaniels, setters, pointers, cockers and springers—each of these distinctions indicate the kind of work the dog is capable of doing. Because of the even temperaments and placidity of these purebred dogs, the group contains many of the most popular of companion dogs as well. Even today many owners of these sporting dogs use them in the field, although most do not. The Cocker Spaniel, Golden Retriever, and Labrador Retriever are without peers as hunting and companion dogs. Persons interested in these dogs should be cautious about choosing the right source. Since popular dogs can become over-abundant and breeders can become careless (and money-minded), you must research your source carefully. Other notable, though less popular, sporting dogs include the English Springer Spaniel, English Cocker Spaniel, Pointer, Weimaraner, Irish Setter and German Shorthaired Pointer.

Hounds: This group includes two

Beagle puppy. If you are going to own a pup, you must realize that the little fellow is going to become a member of your family and an important part of your home life. Photo by Robert Pearcy.

Your own needs, temperament, and lifestyle must be considered when deciding which breed of dog is right for *you*. Borzoi puppy photographed by Isabelle Francais.

kinds of hounds: scent hounds and sight hounds. As implied, a scent hound works off his nose to find his quarry; a sight hound relies on his keen eyes to hunt. Due to the differences in geography and the demands on the dogs, the two kinds of hounds look very different. The scent hounds are essentially smaller, cobby, and thicker of body, often with looser skin. Popular examples of hounds include the Basset Hound, Beagle, Bloodhound, and Dachshund. Each of these familiar canines are also extraordinary companion dogs, despite their nosey expertise. For hunting purposes the Coonhounds (Black and Tan and Redbone) should be mentioned as specialists and hard workers. Among the sight hounds, which are longer of leg, thinner of body, with slender heads, we note the Greyhound, Borzoi, Afghan Hound, Irish Wolfhound and Saluki. Although all the hounds are essentially reticent and well-behaved dogs, the sight hounds are less popular probably because of their larger size. Exercise is a big must for all hounds—the tall ones need to stretch their awesome limbs and the short ones need to keep moving to avoid getting complacently pudgy.

Working Dogs: Versatile and hard-working purebreds outline the union of the working dogs. These wondrous dogs have held various occupations throughout the years: sled pullers, cart pullers, flock guardians, rescue workers, fishermen, tax collectors, night watchmen, etc. As is evident, this is a fascinating group of dogs clumped together because of their talents and strong proclivity to perform specific tasks. The Alaskan Malamute, Samoyed, and Siberian Husky are the nordic members—the sled pullers historically by trade and presently by sport. Rottweilers, Bernese Mountain Dogs, and Giant Schnauzers have been used as cart pullers, though today they are pretty competent guard dogs. The Kuvasz, Komondor and Great Pyrenees epitomize the great flock guard breeds of Europe—for stable temperament and patience, these dogs are unsurpassable. Other multi-talented, handsome dogs in the group include the Doberman Pinscher, Boxer, St. Bernard, Mastiff, and Bullmastiff.

Terriers: This energetic and snappy clan of canines was developed to rid the landscape of destructive vermin. While many terriers today are kept for companions—they're terrific with kids—a good number of terrier breeds have intact rat-killing instincts. The Fox Terriers are among the most recognizable of the terriers, although quite a few breeds maintain strong followings: Miniature Schnauzers, Scottish Terriers, Cairn Terriers, and Airedale Terriers. The British nation is responsible for creating almost all of the terrier breeds, as many of the breeds bear names of British locales: Sealyham, Skye, Norfolk, Staffordshire, Bedlington, West Highland, etc. A little different are the bull and terrier breeds. The Staffordshire Bull Terrier, Bull Terrier, American Staffordshire Terrier and the American Pit Bull Terrier are among these unique, powerful dogs.

Toy Breeds: Dogs for companionship sake, the toy breeds by definition are tiny and cuddly. Practically every nation has developed its own companion breeds. Many of these are the beloved, somewhat spoiled pets of the nobility and affluent; others were extreme bantamization of the popular dogs of the day. The most recognizable of members in this menagerie of miniatures include: the Pekingese, Pomeranian, Chihuahua, Maltese, Silky Terrier, Yorkshire Terrier, Pug, and Cavalier King Charles Spaniel. Among show-dog people, these breeds are very popular, perhaps because these dogs love attention and usually take to the show ring with verve and a naturalness that other dogs can only impersonate! These are ideal apartment dogs and often tend to be one-owner dogs.

Herding Dogs: The dogs in this canine corral are defined by their biddability, intelligence, and obedience. The proverbial companion dog, immortalized in "Lassie," heads the group: the Collie. Slightly smaller, though no less wondrous, the Shetland Sheepdog (affectionately called the Sheltie) joins the ranks. Even more popular is the German Shepherd Dog, used extensively in police work and in the

military. Other great herding dogs include the Bearded Collie, a dog growing in popularity in England and America; the Australian Cattle Dog, the renowned heeler from Down Under; the Cardigan and Pembroke Welsh Corgis; and the blue-eyed Bobtail, the Old English Sheepdog. The Belgian breeds are also noteworthy: the Malinois, Tervuren and Belgian Sheepdogs, each of which are comparable to the beloved German Shepherd Dog.

Non-Sporting Dogs: Not every dog can be the top athlete in his class! The non-sporting dogs have done well to keep off the field and are comprised of truly neat dogs, though they are dogs which don't fit neatly into the other groups. Nonetheless, who can argue with the likes of one of the world's most beloved and wholly unique dogs, the Poodle? The Poodle has the most impressive of all coats in dogdom and is wondrous in its versatility and super-canine intelligence—Poodles historically were great sportsmen, hunting with their great noses and lugging the tubbiest of ducks to shore! Too big for most kennel clubs' toy boxes are the Lhasa Apso, French Bulldog, Bichon Frise, Tibetan Spaniel and Boston Terrier. Yet these snazzy little guys are prime companion dogs and just plain special. Other classic canines are grouped here too: the Bulldog, one of the most easily distinguishable of dogs; Dalmatian, a smart chap in black and white (and sometimes liver and white!); the companionable

Familiarity with the various groups of purebred dogs and their characteristics can enable you to select the kind of dog you really want. The German Shepherd Dog, a member of the herding group, is renowned for his remarkable ability to be trained for a variety of special tasks.

In many instances, a puppy bears small resemblance to its parents. This pair of Old English Sheepdog pups, shown with their mom, have yet to acquire the profuse shaggy coat for which their breed is famous. This OES family, owned by Stan and Sue Mannlein, was photographed by Isabelle Francais.

Chow Chow, of ancient Oriental descent; and also the amazing Chinese Shar-Pei, a purebred of in*creasing*ly growing demand. The Keeshond and Schipperke complete the group's listing.

REGISTRATION PAPERS

If you pay for a purebred dog, make sure that you get his pedigree papers and an application signed by the breeder. You will need these to register your puppy with a kennel club. The people who sell you your pet will help you fill out these important forms. If your dog is not registered, it cannot participate in dog shows, nor can its puppies ever be registered.

Additionally, for your own protection, make an agreement in writing with the seller that he will either refund your money or give you another dog if a veterinarian of your choice does not give the puppy a clean bill of health. Then, take him to the vet for a complete physical examination.

BRINGING THE NEW PUPPY HOME

Bring your puppy home in the daytime, in the morning if possible. This gives him a chance to become acquainted with his new surroundings before it's time to go to bed. His new quarters should be awaiting his arrival. His sleeping accommodations can be a wire cage or a specially designed doggie bed. (If you opt for the wire cage, put a washable cushion or folded blanket at one end and some newspaper at the other end.)

Make up your mind that he is going to be a little lonesome for his mother and siblings. When he starts to whimper, a loving pat on the head and some soothing words should help to settle him down. The old wives' tale which holds that a hot water bottle and a ticking alarm clock will provide comfort for the pup— simulating the warm bodies and beating hearts of his siblings—is still sometimes adhered to by some breeders.

Dogs and cats can be great companions to each other if they are introduced at an early age.

Feeding

Our twentieth-century world places enormous emphasis on efficiency and speed. While the feeding of puppies and dogs once required great effort, today you only need the right information and quality dog-food products. The healthy puppy that you have just acquired and taken into your home is already accustomed to a particular diet, so you must find out from the seller what the puppy has been eating. The more specific the details the better—find out the brand name and variety too! Even if this food isn't your first choice, you must continue with it for about a week, while slowly introducing the new food. This process must be undertaken gradually so as not to upset the puppy's digestive system.While the dog is essentially a carnivore, the dog needs more than just meat products to get proper nutrition. In order to get the desired amounts of protein, carbohydrates, vitamins, minerals and fats, the dog must be provided a well-balanced, sensible and consistent diet.

A puppy is weaned completely from its mother at approximately seven weeks of age. Such a newly weaned pup needs four daily feedings, which include broth-soaked kibble, canned dog food, whole-grained cereals and milk. This feeding schedule continues until the puppy is about twelve weeks old. The pet industry provides terrific options for dog owners, including lines of progressive meals, similar to what is available for growing babies.

During the period from three to six months of age, the pup need only receive three meals per day, essentially one milk and two meat. Once the puppy has reached six months, two meals will do; at one year, one daily meal is sufficient, although you may wish to continue the two-meal schedule to which the dog has grown accustomed. Dietary supplements, such as biscuits and treats, are recommended by most pet experts.

The size of your dog and its growth rate must considered when feeding your pet. Remember that the calorie intake of a quickly growing, high metabolism dog will not be equivalent to a smaller, more sedate breed. Pet shops sell a variety of quality pet foods, all of which are formulated to fulfill the needs of the growing puppy. Such products are fortified with essential vitamins and minerals.

Of course in addition to food, water must be provided. Clean water should always be available to the dog. Refill the bowl several times each day—do not simply add to the stagnant water in the bowl.

The water and food bowls should be kept in a designated place.

It is advisable to feed your puppy his meals at the same regular times each day. Go easy on treats and snacks, as these do not provide the nutritional mainstay of his diet. Photo by Isabelle Francais.

A good diet, regular veterinary care, and your love and attention will make for a healthy, happy puppy. Cairn Terrier pup photographed by Robert Pearcy.

Training

The most important elements in your puppy's training program are consistency, patience, and praise. Don't make the mistake of expecting too much too soon, as this wouldn't be fair to your new puppy.

HOUSEBREAKING

This can begin the day you bring your puppy home. With persistence, housebreaking can be accomplished in two to four weeks, with an occasional lapse for a short time after that. The puppy will usually want to relieve himself about ten minutes after eating. If at all possible, take him outdoors at this time. Until he is about six months old it may be necessary to walk him five times a day. After this it will be possible to reduce the trips to three a day. On these walks he will probably show a preference for a spot which other dogs have used. When he does, walk him to this particular place every time you take him out, and he will soon associate the outings with the idea of relieving himself and will usually do so promptly when he gets to his preferred spot. When he has relieved himself, lavishly praise him and take him right back inside the house. This will impress on him that this is the purpose of the walk.

PAPER TRAINING

Spread out newspapers in a spot that you have designated as your puppy's comfort station. Shortly after the puppy has eaten, take him there and stay with him until he has had his movement, and then praise him highly. In addition, take the puppy to this same spot after he has awakened from his overnight sleep as well as after naps.

Next, remove the soiled newspapers, replacing them with clean ones, leaving one of the soiled papers on top. Or, if you prefer, purchase at your pet shop one of the several housebreaking aids which are made for this purpose. The odor reminds the puppy of what the papers are for.

When you begin paper training, spread the newspapers over a wide area. You will discover that he will return to a preferred spot. Gradually reduce the spread of papers until you have only a few thicknesses spread where he wants them. Scold him when he does make a mistake, then carry him to his comfort station. Under *no* circumstances should a puppy be hit if he has an accident. Scrub the soiled spot immediately with vinegar or ammonia diluted in warm water. This will kill any odor which might attract him back to the same spot.

To make the transition from the

pup's use of newspapers inside to using the great outdoors exclusively, take along a fold of soiled newspaper or a can of a commercial housebreaking aid when you walk him. Spread this on the spot you prefer him to use and if and when he does, praise him profusely. Praise yourself too because you've both done a good job.

GOOD MANNERS

A dog that is well trained is truly a joy to own. It is advisable to begin a training program while your pet is still a puppy; by the time he is an adult dog, he will have learned all of the rules that you have established.

If he has a comfortable spot of his own, your puppy is less likely to choose yours. A stern "No," emphasized with a clap of your hands, will point out his mistake. Your puppy will catch on quickly if you keep at it. Dog repellent sprays are also useful for keeping dogs off furniture. They smell bad to dogs, but not to you, and are harmless when sprayed on upholstery.

Puppy dogs are especially exuberant and will not hesitate to let you know it. When your puppy jumps up on you (or anyone else), clasp his front paws and place them on the floor, at the same time saying "No" sharply.

A puppy is anxious to test his new teeth on almost anything. The best thing that you can do to satisfy your pet's need to chew and to relieve his puppy anxieties is to provide him with an appropriate chew object.

Nylabone® and Gumabone® products, specially designed to satisfy a dog's chewing needs, are safe and effective and will provide endless hours of pleasure and satisfaction for your pet. These products are available in a variety of sizes and designed in interesting shapes: bones, knots, and rings. An important additional benefit is that they promote effective interim tooth cleaning and vigorous gum massage, thus helping to protect your puppy from periodontal disease.

If you discover your puppy chewing on anything other than what he is permitted to have, immediately show your disapproval by firmly saying "No" and taking the forbidden object away from him. Conversely, when he chews on his own things, pet him and lavishly praise him. Make sure that everyone in the household does this consistently.

If your puppy yelps while you're away, your neighbors will let you know about it fast. Their complaints are justified, so take the trouble to break your little canine pal of this habit while there's still time. Make believe you're going away, but wait quietly outside the door. The chances are he'll start to howl as soon as he thinks you've gone. Shout "No, No, No!" and rush back inside, scolding him and making a great display of displeasure. A few lessons like this, before his bad habit becomes ingrained, will teach him that the only thing that results from yelping and barking is an angry master.

A mongrel puppy—one that is of mixed ancestry—can be a good canine companion, but one can only guesstimate what he will look like (and how he will behave) when he is grown up.

Chinese Shar-Pei puppies, wonderful and wondrously wrinkled, enjoying the attention and affection of their young mistress. Alice S. Lawler is the owner of these pups, photographed by Isabelle Francais.

A dog who barks a warning is a valuable companion, but a yapper who barks at any and everything is a nuisance unless he is taught to stop on command.

OBEDIENCE TRAINING

While manners and housebreaking should be taught to your puppy from the day he enters your home, simple obedience commands like those presented here can wait until he's at least six months old. The need for patience when it comes to dog training cannot be overemphasized. With patience goes persistence. If you keep this thought foremost in your mind while you are training your pet, the results are more apt to be successful.

Leash training: Teaching this to a puppy is not difficult, but before you start, get him used to wearing a collar and leash. Get him used to the collar by letting him wear it around the house for a longer time each day. After a couple of days like this, take him on his first walk. Call him to your side, and as you step out say "Heel." This is an obedience command he will have to learn later, so he might just as well get used to it from the start. He probably will want to drag behind or rush ahead and he will plunge and pull against the leash. Continue your walk, however, leading him along with you (and repeating "Heel"). He will quickly learn that it is useless to struggle and more comfortable to come along. When he ceases to struggle, pet him and reward him.

"Come" command: Attach a lightweight cord at least twenty feet long to your puppy's collar—pet shops carry a variety of these items. Allow your pup to have a short romp, then, when his attention is attracted elsewhere, call him by name and give the command "Rover, come!" If he responds, pat him, reward him with a treat, and allow him to continue his romp, repeating the call at intervals. Before long, he may refuse to come when ordered. Grasp the end of the taut cord, repeat the command, and give the cord a sharp tug. He will probably try to resist, but keep giving the command; a few sharp tugs will probably bring him to you. If they don't, pull him in, but reward him anyway. However badly a puppy behaves, never scold him when he comes to you. A dog must always feel that when you say "Come" something good is going to happen.

"Sit" command: With your pup in front of you or by your side, hold the leash taut in your right hand and give the command "Sit." At the same time, lean over and with your left hand gently press down on his rump until he is sitting. He may want to lie down or flop over on his side. Don't let him. Straighten him out with your left hand on his flank. Then give him a treat and praise him. Repeat this routine several times, always rewarding him when he responds. Soon he will associate the command with the pressure on his rump and anticipate it before he is touched.

"Down" command: Once your

puppy sits on command, it is not difficult to teach the "Down" command. With one hand, hold him by the collar, give the command "Down," and gently press down on his rump with the other. As soon as he is in a sitting position, use your right hand to slide his front feet out from under him while you still press down with your left hand. Another way is to pass the leash under your shoe and hold it taut with your right hand while pressing down on his shoulder with your left, at the same time commanding "Down." Give the command "Up" and take a step or two forward when you want him to rise. Repetition of this will soon teach your dog to go down on all fours at the command.

"Stay" command: This command is an extension of the "Sit" and "Down" commands. First, command the puppy to "Sit" or "Down." Face the dog and order him to "Stay." Slowly back away, admonishing him with your upraised finger. If he breaks, give him a sharp "No!" Lay the leash on the ground pointing from him to you as you back away. Keep repeating "Stay" or "No," according to his reaction. At each lesson move farther away until there is an open space between you and the loop of the leash. If he stays only momentarily at first, still praise and reward him when you call him to you.

"Heel" command: This is the correct way to walk a mature dog. The loop of the leash is held in your right hand, the thong passes across your body to the dog who is sitting

on your left; you control the slack of the leash with your left hand, shortening or lengthening it as the case may be. Say clearly, "Rover, heel!" and start out with your left foot. When the dog strains ahead, tug back sharply with your left hand, but then let the leash slacken instantly. The tug on the leash is what does it. It makes him momentarily uncomfortable, and he quickly learns that if he walks correctly at your left knee there will be no tug. Keep walking, keep tugging the leash when needed, and keep repeating "Heel." Some trainers use a rolled-up tube of newspaper to tap the dog whenever they say "Heel," but I have never found it necessary. Patting your left leg often helps, however. Remember to praise him on each return to position. Try this training session fifteen minutes a day, twice a day. You'll be surprised at how quickly he learns.

"Shake hands" command: Puppies paw at each other in play. Your pup will paw at you. Fine. Grab his paw and shake. Wrong paw? Yes, since most pups extend the paw nearest the hand you're using. With the pup in the "Sit" position, push against his right shoulder with your left hand. As his foot comes up, take the paw in your right hand, shake, then reward him. Keep repeating the command "Shake hands" as you rehearse him in the action.

Again, don't expect instant successful results from your new puppy.

Cute, cuddly, and companionable, dog breeds of the toy group have long held a beloved place in the hearts—and laps—of their fanciers. This little charmer is a Bichon Frise, owned by Judith L. Hilmer. Photo by Vince Serbin.

The Doberman Pinscher is known for his highly intelligent and fearless character, a trait which suits him well in his duties as guard dog, watchdog, and police dog. A training program, no matter what breed of dog you choose, is best begun when the animal is a puppy. Photo by Robert Pearcy.

Grooming

A puppy deserves a little special attention at least once a day.

In addition to helping your puppy look his best, the time you spend grooming him will strengthen the bond between you and him.

BRUSHING

Use a soft-bristle brush for a young pup. As he matures, you'll need a stiffer brush or curry comb, and if he's got a long, shaggy coat, a steel comb and wire brush will be needed to untangle the snarls. First, brush with the grain—or growth of the hair—to clean the surface coat. Second, brush against the grain to clean out the undercoat and massage the skin. Finally, brush the hair back to its original position. Use the comb to ease out mats and snarls from longhaired dogs, using a few teeth at one end to work them out. Use the comb, too, for ear fringes, beards, and feathered tails.

BATHING

Dogs need not be bathed except when necessary; never more than once a month, and not even then unless there's some special reason. Choose a warm draft-free place and put several inches of lukewarm water in a fairly deep tub. Use a washcloth without soap on his head and ears. Then, using a shampoo specially formulated for dogs, lather him over from neck to tail, back to paws, including his underbody. Do not let any suds get in his nose, eyes, or ears. After soaping him down thoroughly to the skin, rinse him completely. A spray-hose attachment will come in handy here. It is important to get out every last bit of shampoo.

Then, before you lift the puppy from the tub, wrap him in a big towel.

This will protect you from his natural instinct to shake himself dry. When he is as dry as you can get him, let him romp around in a warm room that is free from drafts. Some pet owners prefer to blow-dry their pet's coat using a blow dryer (heat set on low).

In between baths (or if your puppy needs spot cleaning), you can use a dry shampoo. Available at pet shops, these are easy to use, and highly practical in winter or at times when a tub bath is out of the question.

CARE OF THE EYES

Regularly check your pet's eyes for any signs of irritation. To clean discharge from the corners of the eyes, use only a cotton swab dipped in warm water. If your pup has been running through high weeds and grass, you may find pollen or seeds under the eyelid. Irritated eyes can be treated with a mild boric-acid solution. There are also excellent dog eye-washes available at pet counters. Don't hesitate to see your veterinarian if irritation or inflammation persists.

CARE OF THE EARS

Wax build-up in your puppy's ears can be prevented by regular cleaning. Do not use soap and water on them, however. Use a special ear-cleaning solution available at pet shops or from your veterinarian. Be gentle and avoid probing deeply into the ear; instead, clean only the outer surface areas.

If your pet repeatedly scratches at his ears or shakes his head, he may have an infestation of ear mites. An ear mite medicament should clear up this problem.

CARE OF THE TEETH

You can help to prevent plaque and tartar build-up on your puppy's teeth by offering him the appropriate chew items. Nylabone® products, available at pet shops, are specially designed to keep your puppy's teeth

and gums clean and healthy, in addition to serving as an enjoyable outlet for your pet's need to chew.

CARE OF THE FEET

Carefully examine your puppy's feet after outdoor excursions. Prompt attention should be given to any cut or abrasion on the paw pads.

If the nails are allowed to grow too long, they may cause discomfort and possibly lameness. But if they are kept trimmed, or the dog is given regular exercise on hard pavements to keep them worn down, there should be no problem. Tar, gum, and similar sticky substances may be removed from the puppy's paws by using acetone or nail-polish remover. To clip the nails, use a guillotine-type dog nail clipper. When clipping your puppy's nails, be careful not to cut into the quick (the vein that runs the length of the nail) and draw blood. If this does happen, the blood flow can usually be stopped with a styptic pencil.

The time and effort that you devote to grooming your new pup will be more than compensated for by the attention and affection that he gives you.

A Cocker Spaniel puppy, one of the most popular of all dog breeds, and his pal. Adult supervision is recommended when children and their canine companions play together. Photo by Robert Pearcy.

The type and length of your puppy's coat will determine what kind of grooming program you should implement. Naturally, the longer and more elaborate the coat, the more time will be needed for grooming. Yorkshire Terrier pups owned by Beryl Hesketh and photographed by Isabelle Francais.

Health

With proper attention and care, your puppy should be a healthy and happy pet. But sometimes, even the best-cared-for puppy can contract an illness or disease. In addition, your little canine pal is a veritable bundle of energy whose uncontrolled excitement and enthusiasm can lead him into situations that result in accidental injury. The following discussion is presented to help you familiarize yourself with some of the basics of canine medical care.

FIRST AID

The first thing you should *not* do is to rush to the injured animal and gather him up in your arms. An injured dog is in pain, and he may snap at and even bite those he loves. If he is a small dog, obtain a blanket or a similarly heavy piece of material, fold it into double thickness and drop it over the injured animal. Then gather it round him and carefully pick him up. Do not do this, however, if it is obvious that a bone has been broken. A pup of a large breed may need an emergency muzzle. Take a strip of strong cloth about a yard long and a few inches wide. Make a loop in the center and slip this over his jaws, tightening the knot under his chin. Then bring the ends back over his head and tie them securely behind his ears.

Shock: A badly injured dog may go into shock, and this should be treated immediately. Shock symptoms are a weak but rapid pulse, lethargy, and weakness. The victim is conscious but seems unaware of what is going on. Keep the dog warm. Put a blanket over him, and, if possible, take him indoors. Smelling salts can be used.

Cuts and scratches: Even a small cut or scratch deserves antiseptic. You may wish to trim the hair around the wound to allow air to get to it. If the injured area appears inflamed, or if the pup exhibits a great deal of discomfort, a trip to the veterinarian is in order.

Poisoning: A poisoned dog should be treated as soon as possible. If your pet has ingested gasoline, kerosene, an acid or alkali, milk can be given to dilute the poison and then the animal should be taken to the vet. With substances other than those noted above, vomiting can be induced. The easiest way to do this is with hydrogen peroxide. Use regular household strength (3%) mixed with an equal part of water. Give him a teaspoonful of this mixture for every five pounds he weighs.

Peroxide turns into oxygen and water in the stomach and is harmless. The pup will vomit in about two minutes. After his stomach settles, give him a solution of Epsom salts (a teaspoonful dissolved in water). This will quickly empty the bowels.

If you know what the poison was, and its antidote, you can give the puppy that instead. Peroxide is an antidote for phosphorus, which is often used in rat poisons. Epsom salts is an antidote for lead poisoning, frequently caused by paint or paint odors.

MINOR AILMENTS

The more familiar you are with your puppy's normal appearance and behavior, the easier you will be able to tell when he has a problem. Following is a listing of some of the most common ailments and afflictions that occur in dogs.

Skin Diseases: Differentiating between eczema, mange, ringworm, and other skin diseases is a job for the professional. Small skin lesions can be treated with a general purpose skin remedy, available at your pet shop. But if the problem persists, seek expert advice. *Caution*: Some skin diseases are transmissible to humans, so wash your hands thoroughly after handling a dog with a skin ailment.

Fleas: This problem must be attacked on two fronts. You have not only to rid your puppy of the fleas and eggs infesting his body, you must also exterminate the eggs which have dropped off in his living and sleeping quarters. Use a good commercially prepared flea powder or aerosol spray, following the directions on the container. Then,

completely disinfect his living quarters and bed. This done, go over the pup with a brush and fine-toothed comb to get rid of all the dead or dying parasites. Never neglect an infestation of any parasite; it can be the cause of serious skin trouble.

Ticks: When engorged with blood, these look like very small purplish brown grapes. They cling to the pup's skin and inside his ears. Dab them with a cotton swab dipped in alcohol or petroleum jelly. This loosens their hold and they can be plucked off with tweezers. Grasp the tick firmly at the point where its head is embedded in the skin. This ensures that the tick's mouth parts have not been left behind to cause infection. Peroxide makes a good antiseptic.

Worms and Worming: Even the best-cared-for dogs are subject to worms. But not all worms are the same. There are roundworms, hookworms, whipworms, and tapeworms, to name a few. Each requires its own special treatment. Your veterinarian can recommend the best course of treatment for your puppy. Some common symptoms of worm infestation include: the actual appearance of the worms or worm segments in the bowel movements or vomit; a "pot-belly," diarrhea, persistent vomiting, runny eyes and nose. Dragging the rump on the floor is *sometimes* an indication, but this can also mean that there is an accumulation of secreted matter in the pup's anal glands.

An important part of your dog's overall health is the condition of his teeth and gums. A simple and proven effective method of maintaining your pet's dental hygiene is to provide him with Nylabone® products such as a Nylabone® or Gumabone®. Nancy Strouss is the owner of this young Golden Retriever, photographed by Isabelle Francais.

Bright-eyed, alert, and beautifully coated, this pair of Siberian Husky pups projects every outward sign of good canine health. Carolyn S. Duryea is the owner of these youngsters, photographed by Isabelle Francais.

Ear Canker: A brown, waxy substance in your puppy's ear may indicate trouble ahead. Clean out the ears with a medicated ear-wash available at pet shops or from a veterinarian. If your pup continues to scratch his ears frequently, see your veterinarian for advice.

Constipation: Improper diet is usually the cause of this malady. Change your puppy's menu. Give him more roughage: vegetables, kibble, dog biscuits. (It goes without saying that water must be available to the pup.)

Diarrhea: This is frequently the result of an incorrect diet, although it can sometimes be the symptom of something more serious. An anti-diarrhetic, given in a dosage of two teaspoonsful per ten pounds of body weight, can be administered. A bland diet, consisting of a mixture of cooked lean meat (such as chicken) and cooked white rice, can also help to alleviate the problem.

When a puppy suffers from either constipation or diarrhea, it is a good idea to check on whether he has been chewing some foreign matter. Wood, rubber, plastic, wicker, foam rubber, paper, and carpet are some of the possible culprits.

OTHER HEALTH CONSIDERATIONS

There may come a time when your puppy is listless, doesn't want to eat, and doesn't look his usual bright-eyed self. This might be just an off-day for him, or it could be a sign that he's coming down with something. Watch him carefully. Keep him warm. Don't tire him, and do everything to tempt his appetite.

Temperature: The dog's normal temperature, taken rectally, is 101 to 102°F. If it goes higher and stays high for 24 hours, consider it a danger signal. To take his temperature, place him on a table. Coat the bulb end of a rectal thermometer with petroleum jelly. Raise the dog's tail, and gently insert the thermometer for half its length into the rectum. Leave it there for about two minutes.

After using it you will, of course, disinfect it immediately and shake it down.

Inoculation: Today the science of immunization has developed to a remarkable degree. Puppies can be given long-lasting immunity when they are ten weeks old. Before that, they can be given a temporary immunization. At the same time your vet gives your puppy distemper shots, he will also immunize him against hepatitis and leptospirosis.

Distemper: True distemper occurs less frequently today, thanks to our advanced methods of immunization. However, the word distemper is frequently used in a generic sense to indicate a dog with a generalized set of symptoms. Used in this way, the prognosis might vary from good to fair to poor, depending on what is actually causing the symptoms. There are a number of problems occurring in puppies, the symptoms of which, particularly in their early stages, are very similar.

Some, but by no means all, puppies are left with aftereffects which might range from hardly noticeable to severe, but many do make a complete recovery. Should it turn out that it wasn't true distemper after all, but one of the other puppy ailments, the chances are good for a complete recovery.

Tracheobronchitis: This condition is frequently called kennel cough, and is a common and contagious ailment of puppies. The puppy seems normal in every way except for a dry hacking cough. Fortunately, the dog usually recovers, although the cough may persist for as long as six weeks. Your veterinarian can prescribe the medication necessary to ease the discomfort of kennel cough.

Hepatitis: Drowsiness, vomiting, loss of appetite, high temperature, and great thirst are signs of hepatitis. Sometimes these signs are accompanied by swellings of the head, neck, and abdomen. An annual booster shot is needed after the initial series of puppy shots.

Leptospirosis: This disease is contracted by the dog's licking substances contaminated by the urine of an infected dog or an infected rat. Symptoms of leptospirosis are vomiting, weakness, and a yellowish discoloration of the jaws, teeth, and tongue, indicative of kidney malfunction. Fortunately, your pet can receive an inoculation to protect him from this disease.

Bibliography

ATLAS OF DOG BREEDS
By Bonnie Wilcox and
Chris Walkowicz
TFH H-1091
The ultimate dog breed identification guide, this book traces the history of every recognized dog breed.
Hardcover, 9½ x 12½", 912 pages, over 1100 full-color photos.

ENCYCLOPEDIA OF
DOG BREEDS
By Ernest H. Hart
TFH H-927
A comprehensive reference source on different kinds of dogs and their maintenance and care.
Hard cover, 5½ x 8½", 783 pages, 537 black and white photos, 138 color photos.

HOW TO SHOW YOUR OWN DOG
By Virginia Tuck Nichols
TFH PS-607
All you need to know to get started in dog shows is presented in this informative and easy-to-follow book.
Hard cover, 8½ x 5½", 254 pages, 136 black and white photos, 10 line illustrations.

DOG OWNER'S ENCYCLOPEDIA
OF VETERINARY MEDICINE
By Allen H. Hart, B.V.Sc.
TFH H-934
This book discusses the symptoms and cures of most diseases of dogs.
Hard cover, 5½ x 8", 186 pages, 86 black and white photos.